watch the falling

autumn leaves

Big trees, little trees
climbing high,
leaves stretched up
towards the sky.

Trees lived on Earth long before dinosaurs did.

Apples, bananas, hazelnuts, mangoes, coconuts, cherries...

Contents

The biggest trees in the world are the giant sequoias in the USA. One tree is so big that an arch has been cut through the trunk and cars drive through it!

...all these foods come from trees.

seed

I know wha

There are three main types of tree in the world:

I know that trees have leaves and branches, but what else is there to know?

leaves

bark

roots

You often find palm trees by beaches in hot countries.

Palm trees

These trees are found in hot places. They have big, thick leaves that protect them from hot winds.

Trees are the biggest plants in the world. Most of them grow much taller than us.

4

a tree is!

palm trees, coniferous trees, and deciduous trees.

Trees live much longer than we do. The oldest tree is over 4,000 years old and lives in California, USA.

Coniferous trees

These trees have long, thin leaves called needles, and cones instead of flowers. They keep their leaves all year round.

Conifer

Fir cone

Deciduous trees

These trees have large, flat leaves. They produce flowers in spring and they lose their leaves in winter.

All trees have a trunk, leaves, branches, and long roots that stretch out underground.

5

Now that it has grown, the oak tree makes its own **acorns.** Many acorns will be eaten by squirrels, but some will grow into trees.

The life of a tree

Have you ever seen acorns on an oak tree? These are its seeds. Every tree has seeds, which are **pocket-sized** plants, waiting to grow into more trees.

The seed

Trees grow from seeds. The seeds of an oak tree are called acorns.

3 days old

A seed will start to grow if it has air, water, and warmth.

3 weeks old

The new leaves soak up sunlight, which the tree turns into food.

Young

3 days old

6

Food factories

The leaves on the tree are its food factory. They stretch towards the Sun and use the sunlight to help make food, which they pass down to the rest of the tree in the sap.

Believe it or not, the maple syrup that you put on your pancakes is sap from the sugar maple tree!

Spring

In spring the Sun comes out and the new, strong leaves burst from their buds. This tree also grows flowers, often called blossom, which produce seeds.

A tree for all seasons

Some trees have leaves that change colour in the **autumn** and then drop off. These are the deciduous trees that sleep in winter.

Leaves spread out over the summer months and use sunlight to make food for the tree.

In the spring, trees grow buds that will turn into leaves.

new leaves

the bud

10

Frosty snowflakes settle on the branches.

Winter

The tree uses the food that the leaves have made over the summer to live on through the cold winter. It stands bare waiting for the warm spring months.

As the summer ends, the days get shorter and shorter. This is how the trees know to begin getting ready for **winter**.

old leaves

In the autumn there is less sun and the leaves stop making food. They dry out, which changes their colour.

In the winter there are no leaves making food, but the tree is still alive and preparing to make new buds for the spring.

no leaves

The weather gets colder in autumn and the leaves turn amazing reds, browns, and oranges. The leaves die and begin to fall to the ground.

Autumn

The most famous conifers in the world are Christmas trees. Each year thousands of people bring a tree into their house during December and decorate it.

decorations

Many Christmas tree decorations – wooden and cardboard ones – are also made from trees.

leaves

Conifers have needle-shaped leaves that are thin and hard so that they don't get damaged by the snow.

Although people have been decorating trees for thousands of years, the Germans were the first to bring a pine tree indoors at Christmas.

Christmas trees are grown on tree farms.

Pine trees are triangle-shaped to make sure that as many leaves as possible catch the low-down sun to take in food

Big trees give lots of shade.

Summer

In summer the days are long and the tree is full of leaves working to make food. The flowers turn into seeds, ready to fall and grow into new trees.

pine tree

12

Many insects live inside trees, just under the bark.

The longhorn and deathwatch beetles can harm trees by eating the bark...

...they even like to eat through your wooden furniture!

death-watch beetle

ant

grub

long-horn beetle

Life in a tree

It's not just us that like trees. There are many other **creatures** that use trees too, in lots of different ways

chip-munk

Animals live in trees and also eat the leaves, nuts, fruit, and seeds.

caterpillar

Look at trees in your area in spring time, you may spot birds' nests in the branches.

rees

f you travel to the
old places of the world you
will often find conifer forests.
These trees are evergreen.

cone

seeds

Conifers don't
have flowers.
Instead they have cones
that hold seeds. When a
cone falls it is often open
and the seeds have
dropped out.

Conifers like hot and cold weather

Conifers live in hot places too, but grow particularly well in chilly places.

Evergreen means that the
trees keep their leaves all
year round. They don't
lose them in the winter.

Conifer leaves are
called needles.

13

snake

Many snakes live in trees, so watch out!

butterfly

bat

frog

jaguar

The jaguar snoozes on branches. Its coat helps it hide in the trees so that no animals can see it.

orang-utan

These apes make nests in the trees to sleep in. They leap from tree to tree to find food.

These lizards live in trees above water.

iguana

Trees grow best in rainy places. Some places have so much **rain** that all you can see is trees. These areas are called rainforests.

The rainforest trees are used by hundreds of animals. Jungles are giant animal cities.

A life without trees

shutter   **window**

Look around your home and try to imagine a life without trees. It wouldn't be just your **garden** that would look different.

Tables, chairs, building bricks, cupboards, favourite books – are they made from trees?

Trees all around

It's not just your pencil that is made of wood. Rubbers also come from trees – they are made from sap.

pencils

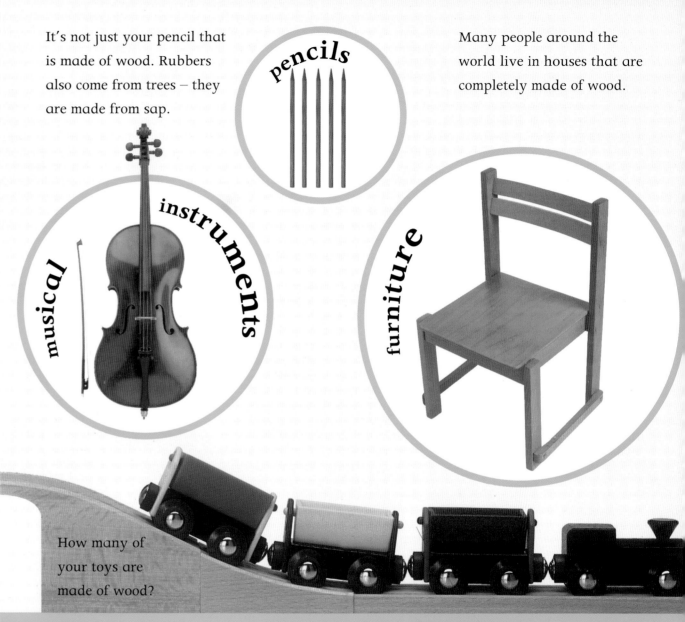

Many people around the world live in houses that are completely made of wood.

staircase

A lot of your house is made of wood too. Floorboards, stairs, and many ceiling beams are wooden.

musical instruments

furniture

toilet paper

toys

How many of your toys are made of wood?

If there were no trees, you wouldn't even have any toilet paper! It's made from pulped-up wood.

Some musical instruments are made from wood – such as violins, clarinets, and pianos.

Wood comes from trees. So if there were
no trees you wouldn't have any **wooden**
furniture, or doors, or even books – they are
made from wood too.

house

decoration

door

What would your
garden or local
park look like
without trees?

19

DK

LONDON, NEW YORK, MUNICH,
MELBOURNE, and DELHI

Written and edited by
Penelope Arlon
Designed by
Tory Gordon-Harris

DTP Designer Almudena Díaz
Production Claire Pearson
Publishing managers
Sue Leonard and Jo Connor

First published in Great Britain in 2006 by
Dorling Kindersley Limited
80 Strand, London, WC2R 0RL

A Penguin Company

2 4 6 8 10 9 7 5 3 1

A CIP catalogue record for this book is available from
the British Library.

ISBN-13: 978-1-4053-1310-0
ISBN-10: 1-4053-1310-2

Colour reproduction by Media Development
and Printing, United Kingdom
Printed and bound in China by
Hung Hing Printing Co., Ltd

Discover more at
www.dk.com

Bonsai **tree**